TEETH AND FANGS

Ray James

Publishing LLC

Vero Beach, Florida 32964

www.rourkepublishing.com

PHOTO CREDITS: All photos © Lynn M. Stone

Title page: A hippo's lower canine teeth are called tusks.

Editor: Robert Stengard-Olliges

Cover design by Nicola Stratford.

Library of Congress Cataloging-in-Publication Data

James, Ray.
  Teeth and fangs / Ray James.
      p. cm. — (Let's look at animals)
  Includes index.
  ISBN 1-60044-174-2 (Hardcover)
  ISBN 1-59515-529-5 (Softcover)
  1. Teeth—Juvenile literature. 2. Fangs—Juvenile literature. I. Title.
II. Series: James, Ray. Let's look at animals.
  QL858.S767 2007
  591.47—dc22
                        2006012629

Printed in the USA

CG/CG

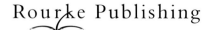

Rourke Publishing

www.rourkepublishing.com – sales@rourkepublishing.com
Post Office Box 3328, Vero Beach, FL 32964

Table of Contents

Teeth

Just like you, many animals have teeth in their jaws. Teeth grow to be very hard. But teeth wear out.

The jaws of some animals, like alligators, replace old teeth. An alligator may have 2,000 teeth during its life.

Teeth Are Tools

Teeth are important tools for an animal. Teeth help animals defend themselves. Teeth help animals clean themselves.

Sharks have very sharp teeth.

Most important, teeth help animals eat. Animals must eat to stay alive.

Animal teeth often gather food. Some animal teeth catch food. Some move food from place to place.

Different Teeth

Many animals with teeth have a mix of different kinds.

Each has a different size and shape. Each has a special use.

Many animals eat plants. Some of their teeth are flat or wide. They cut and chew plants. Cows chew grass.

13

Teeth may stab or tear. They may cut, crush, or chew.

Beavers eat bark and leaves. Their long front teeth cut trees down to make dams.

15

Predators

Some animals eat other animals. These animals are meat-eaters, or **predators**.

At least some of a predator's teeth are sharp. Sharp teeth grab and kill. Wolves, tigers, lions, otters, and badgers are predators.

Furry meat-eaters have **incisor** teeth to grab, bite, and cut.

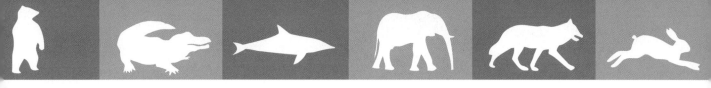

Their long, sharp **canine** teeth stab and kill. **Molars** chew and cut food up.

19

Unusual Teeth

Rattlesnakes have long, hollow teeth called fangs.
Rattlesnakes push poison through their fangs.

Elephants have the largest teeth. Their **tusks** are long teeth. The largest known tusk weighed 258 pounds (117 kilograms).

Glossary

canine (KAY nine) — sharp front teeth often used to bite or stab

incisor (in SIZH ur) — a type of mammal tooth often used for cutting

molar (MOHL ar) — a type of flat tooth used largely for chewing or crushing

predator (PRED uh tur) — an animal that hunts and kills other animals for food

tusk (TUHSK) — a tooth that grows extra large and reaches out of a mammal's mouth

Index

FURTHER READING

Lynch, Wayne. *Whose Teeth Are These?* Gareth Stevens Audio, 2003.
Wormell, Christopher. *Teeth, Tails, and Tentacles*. Running Press Kids, 2004.

WEBSITES TO VISIT

http://www.earthlife.net/mammals/teeth.html
http://www.k12.de.us/warner/teeth.html

ABOUT THE AUTHOR

Ray James writes children's fiction and nonfiction. A former teacher, Ray understands what kids like to read. Ray lives in Gary, Indiana with his wife and three cats.